Flowers

~ Facts on Flowers~

In 17 century Holland Tulip bulbs were more valuable than gold!

The tulip symbolizes immortality, life and love.

Tulip bulbs can be substituted for onions in a recipe.

The lotus was considered a sacred flower by ancient Egyptians.

They viewed it as a symbol of resurrection and eternal life.

Roses are related to apples, raspberries, cherries, peaches, plums nectarines, pears and almonds.

The juice from bluebell flowers was historically used to make glue.

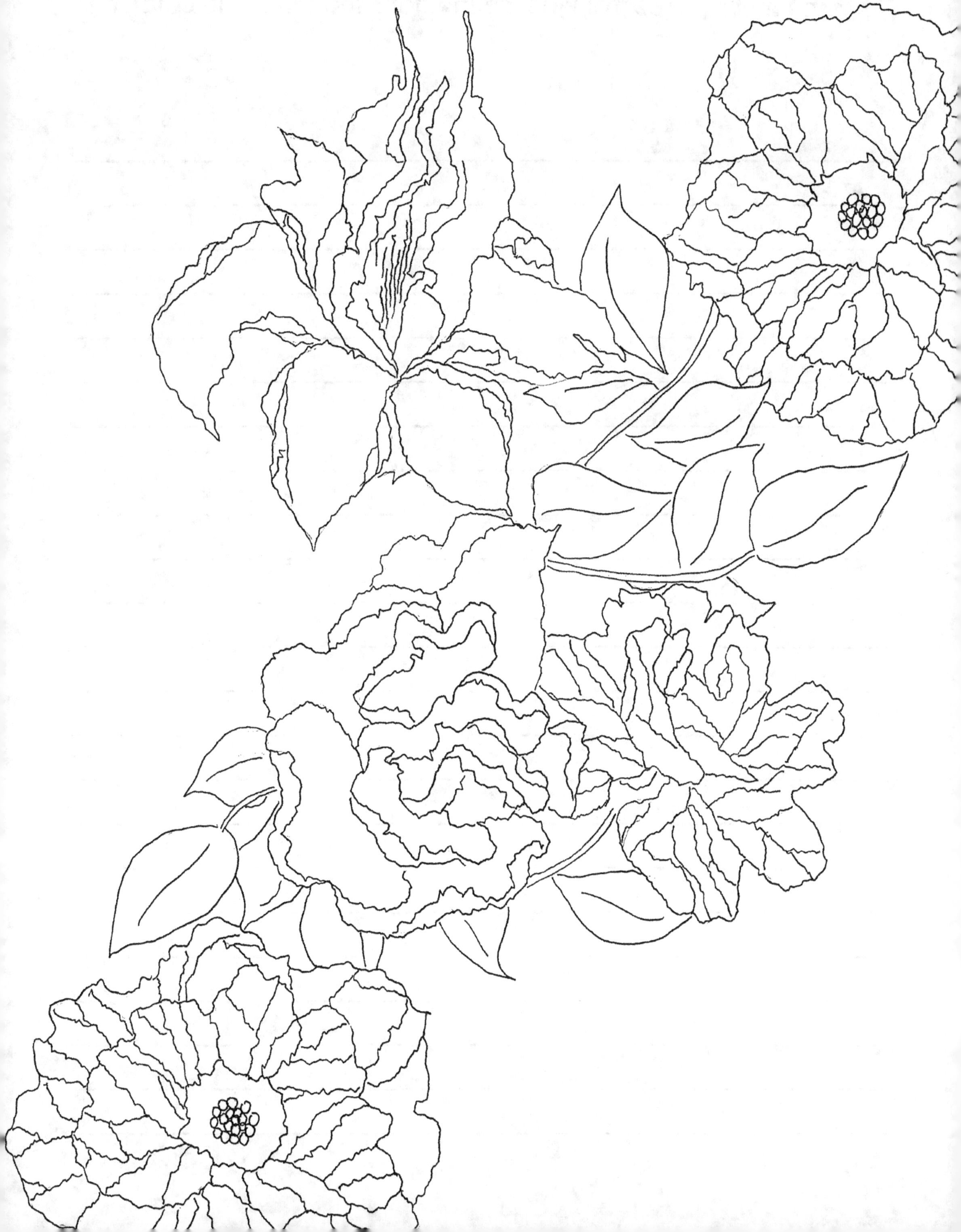

Find inner peace from journaling your thoughts and coloring.

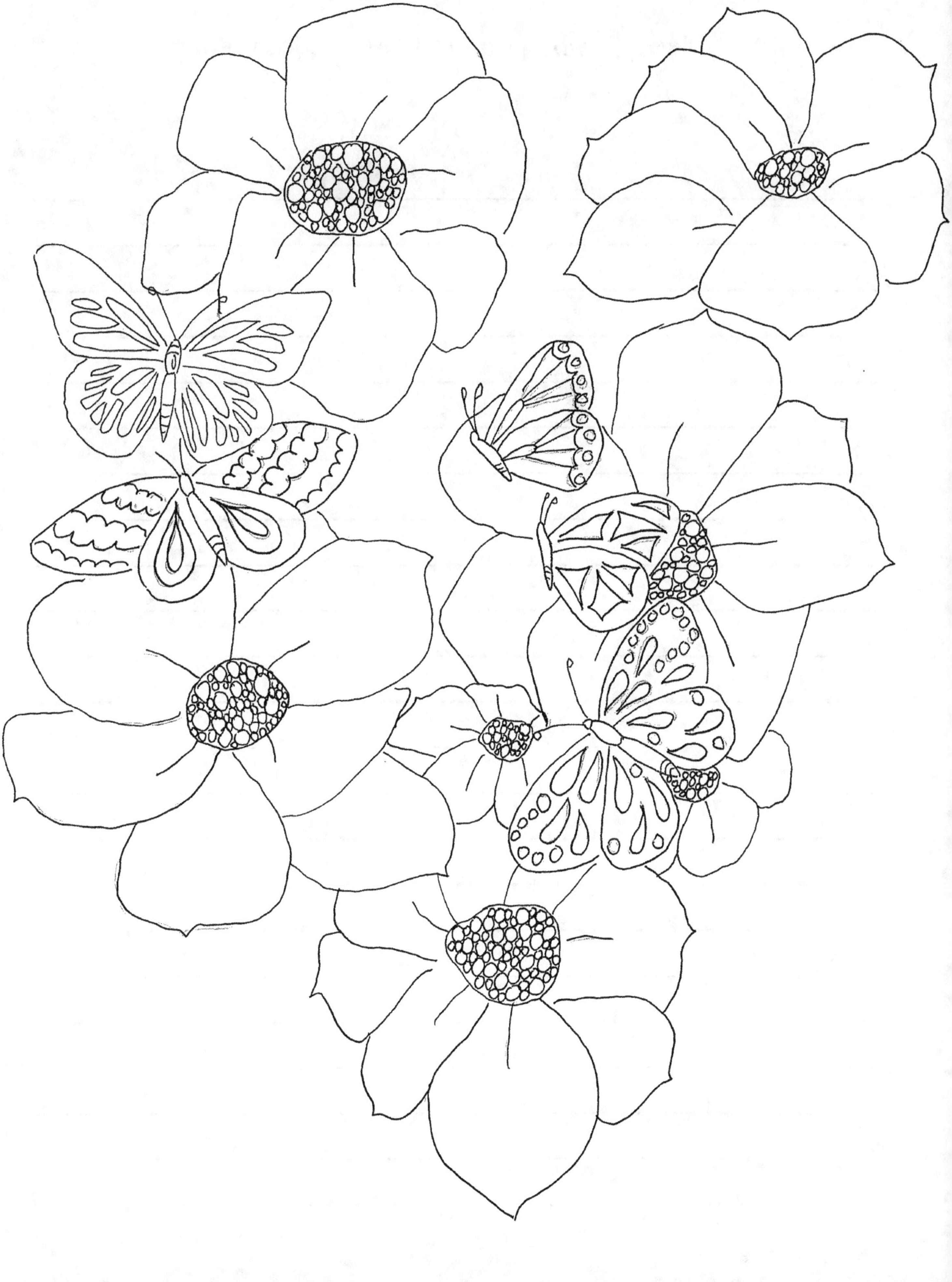

Discover who you really are by journaling.

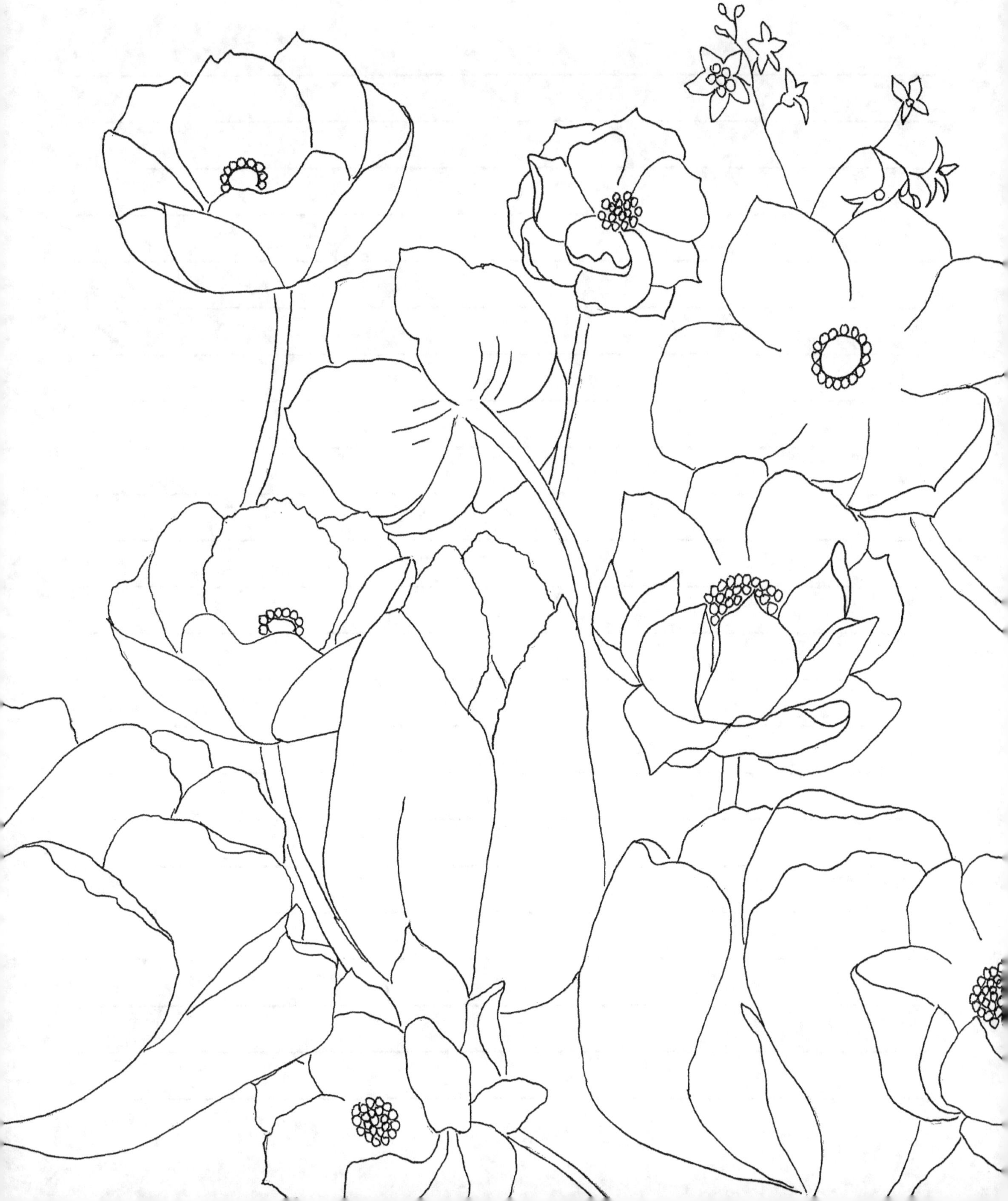

Keep a baby journal when you or a loved one is pregnant.

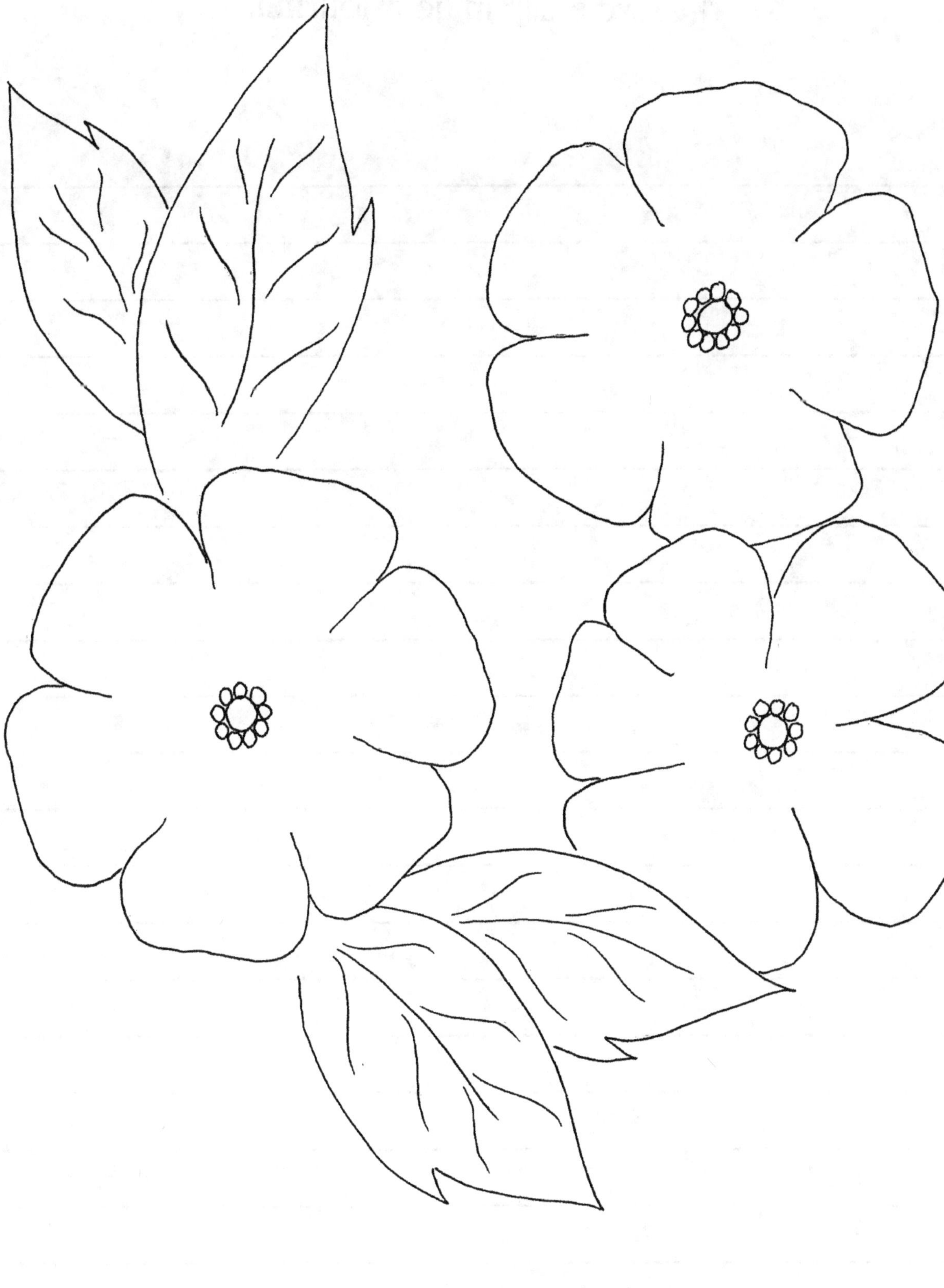

Record a trip in your journal.

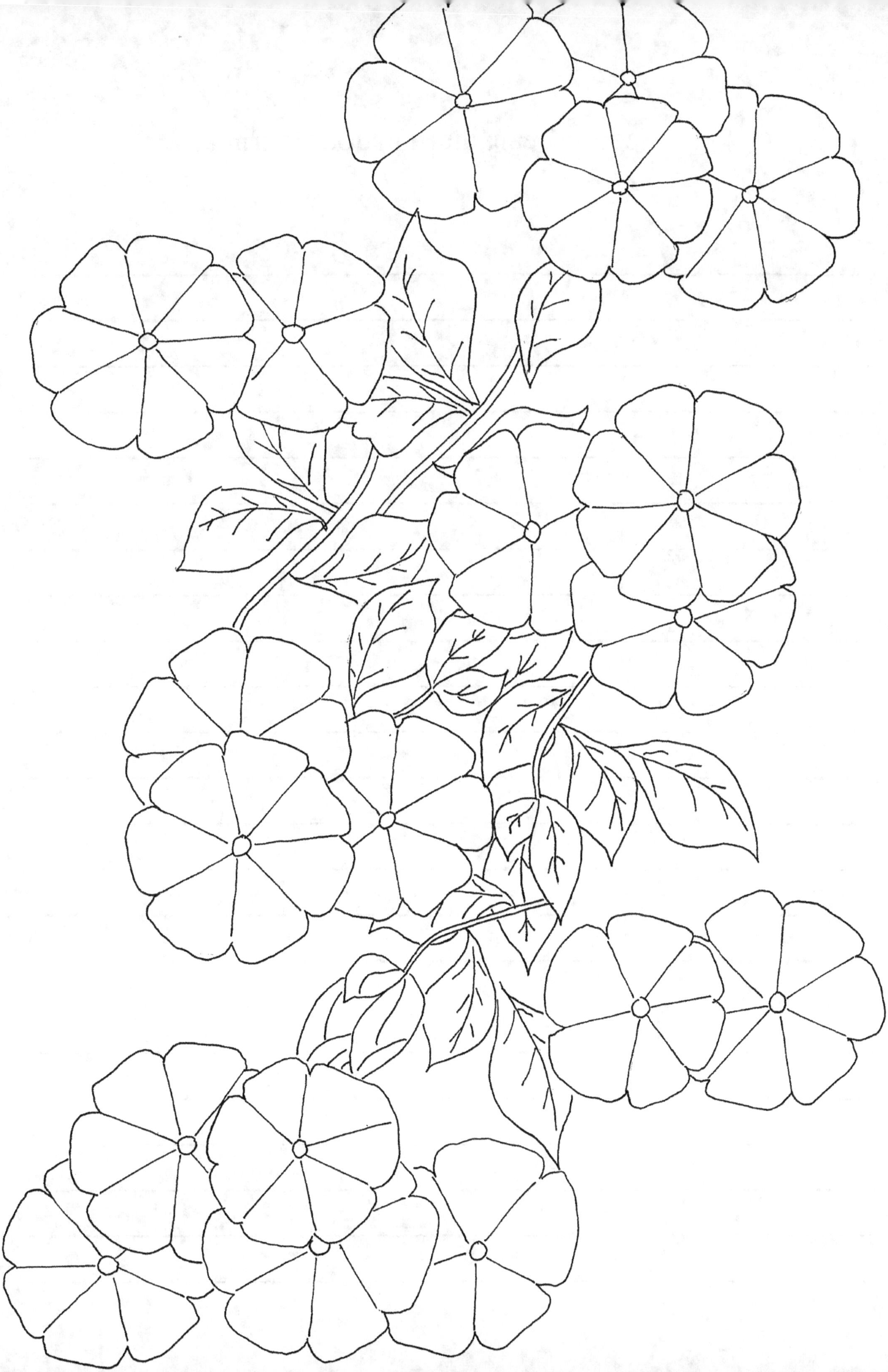

Keep a dream diary in your journal.

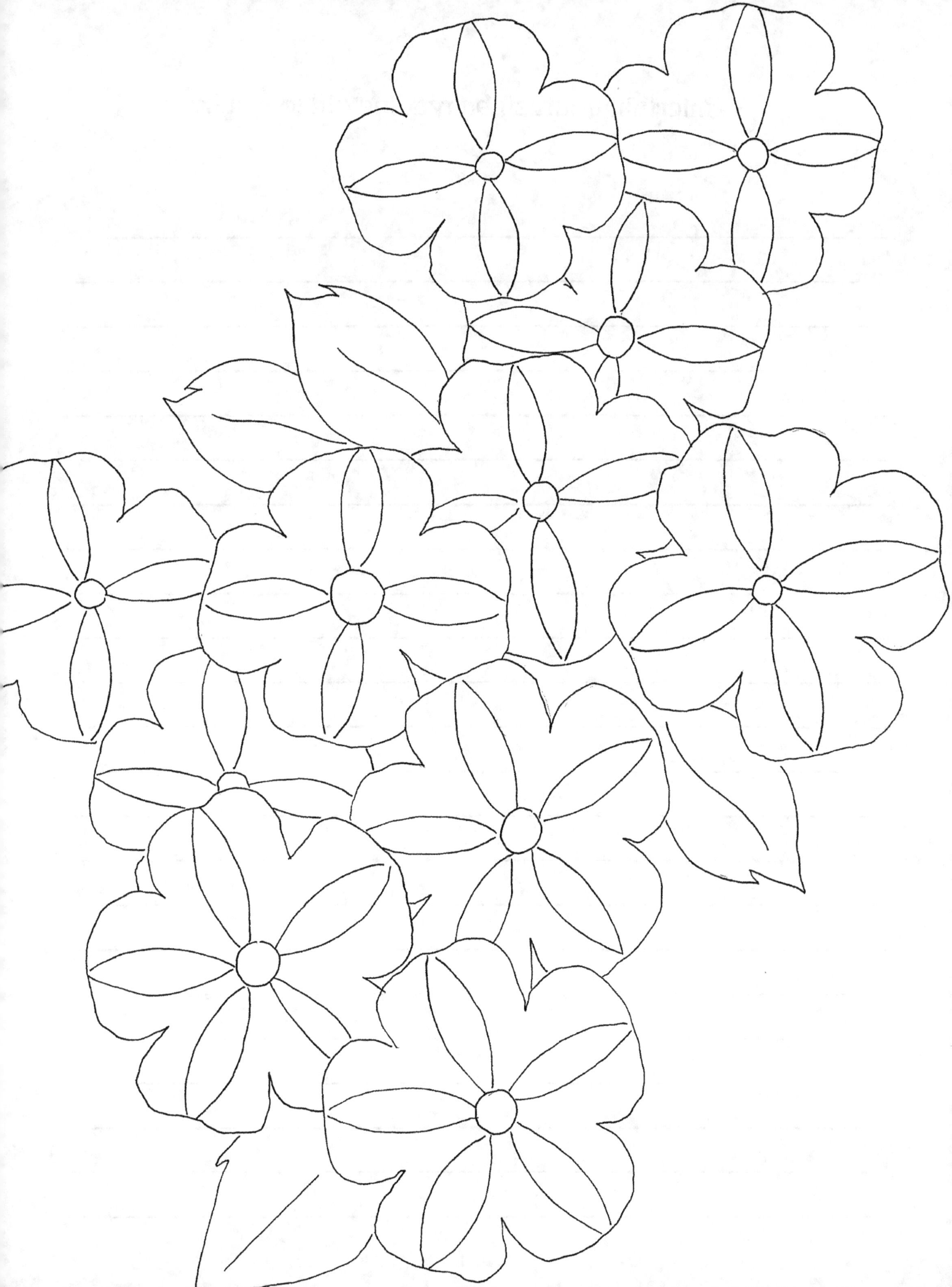

Entertain yourself by reading old journals.

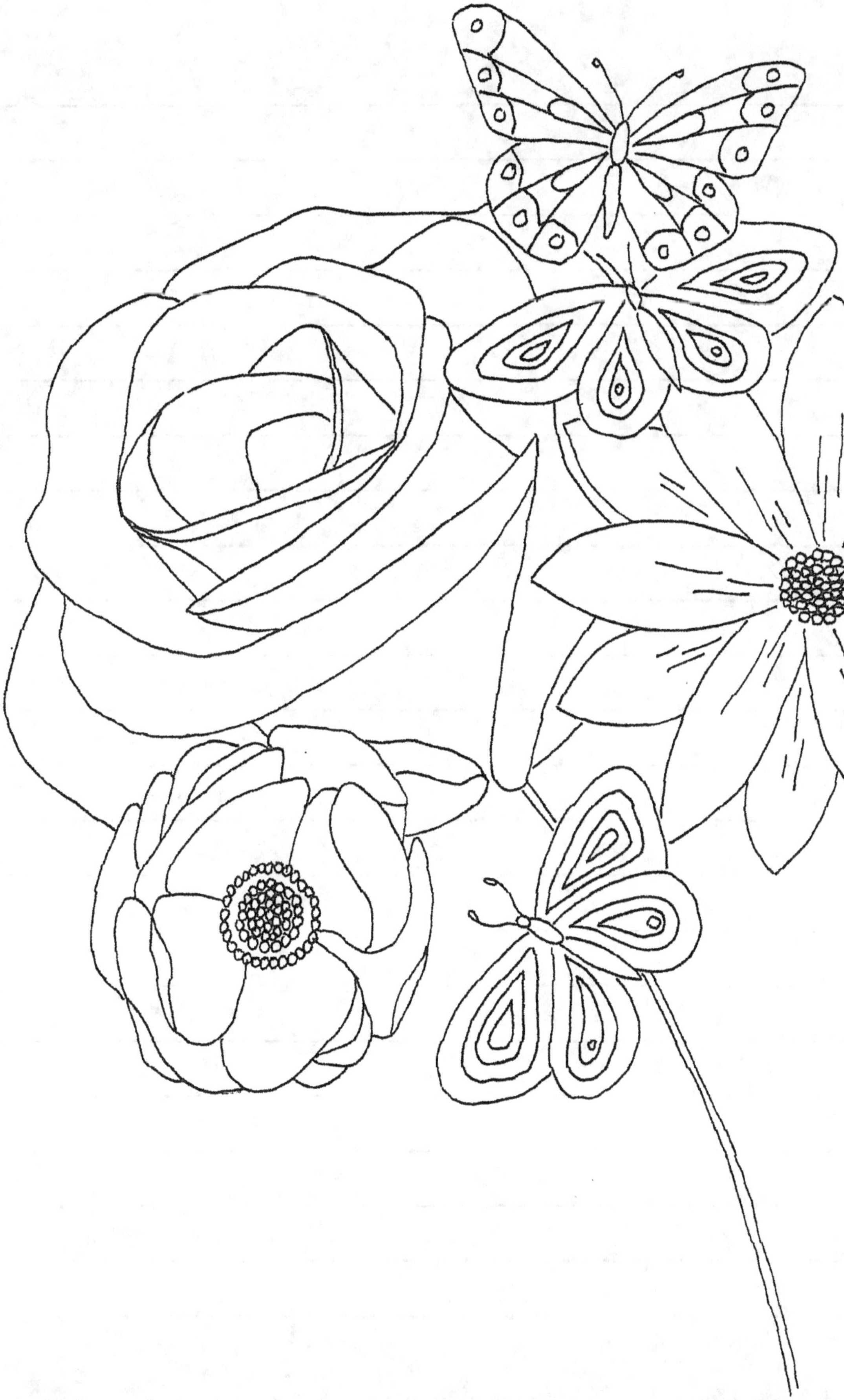

Record quotes, phrases and sayings you want to remember in your journal.

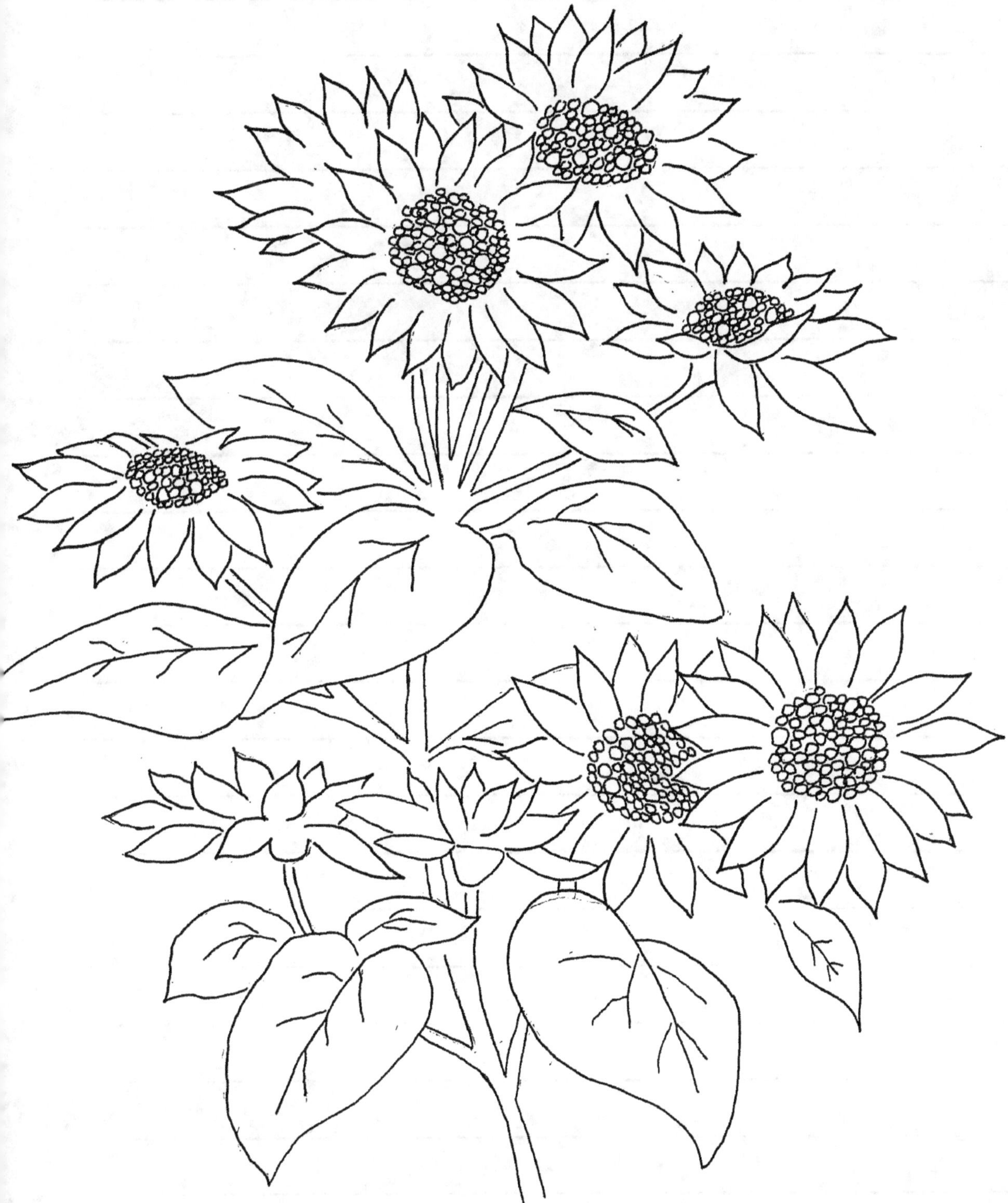

Keep track of favorite scriptures in your journal.

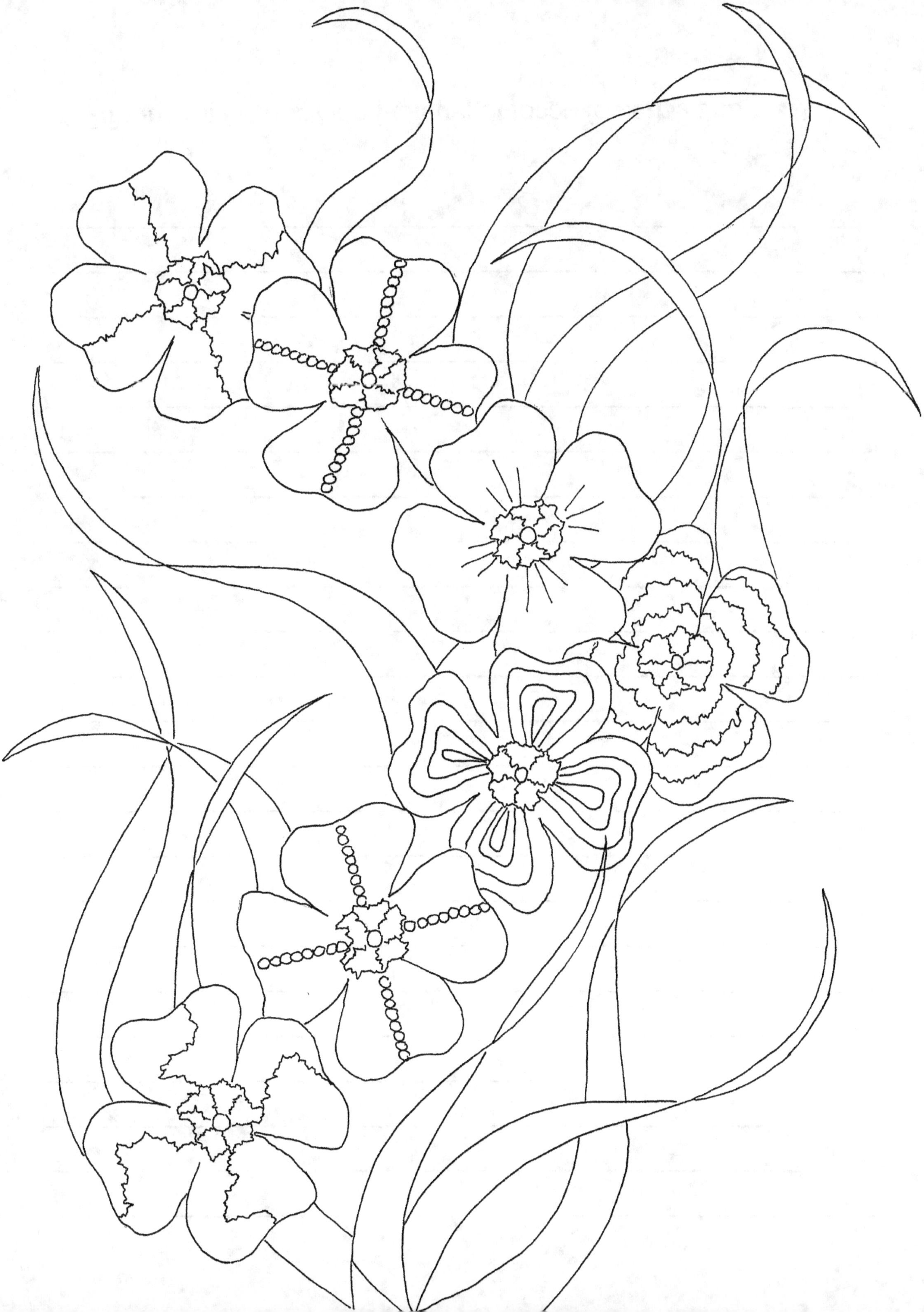

A unique sense of accomplishment comes from journaling.

Develop gratitude for the small things in your journal.

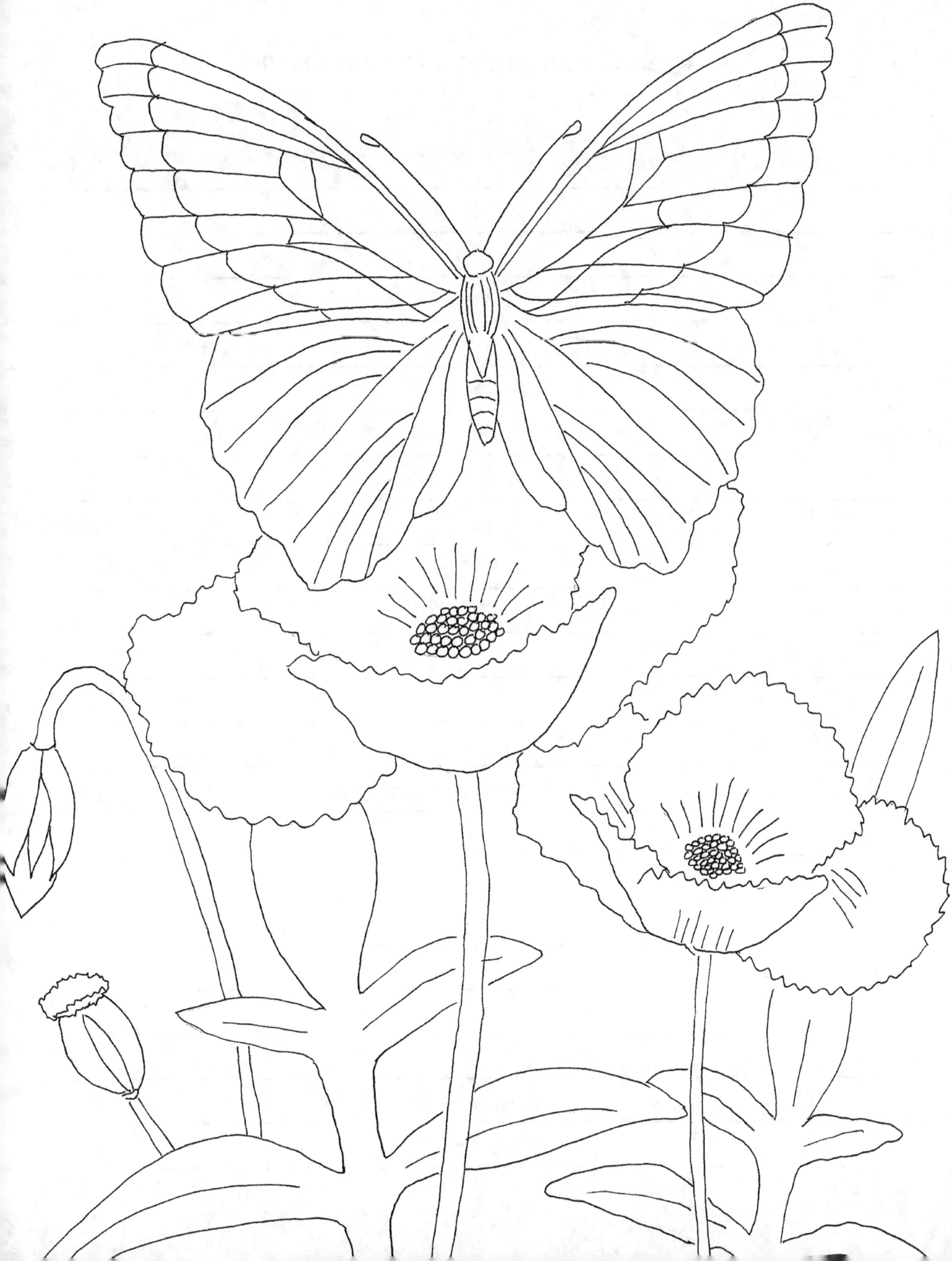

Record your prayers in your journal.

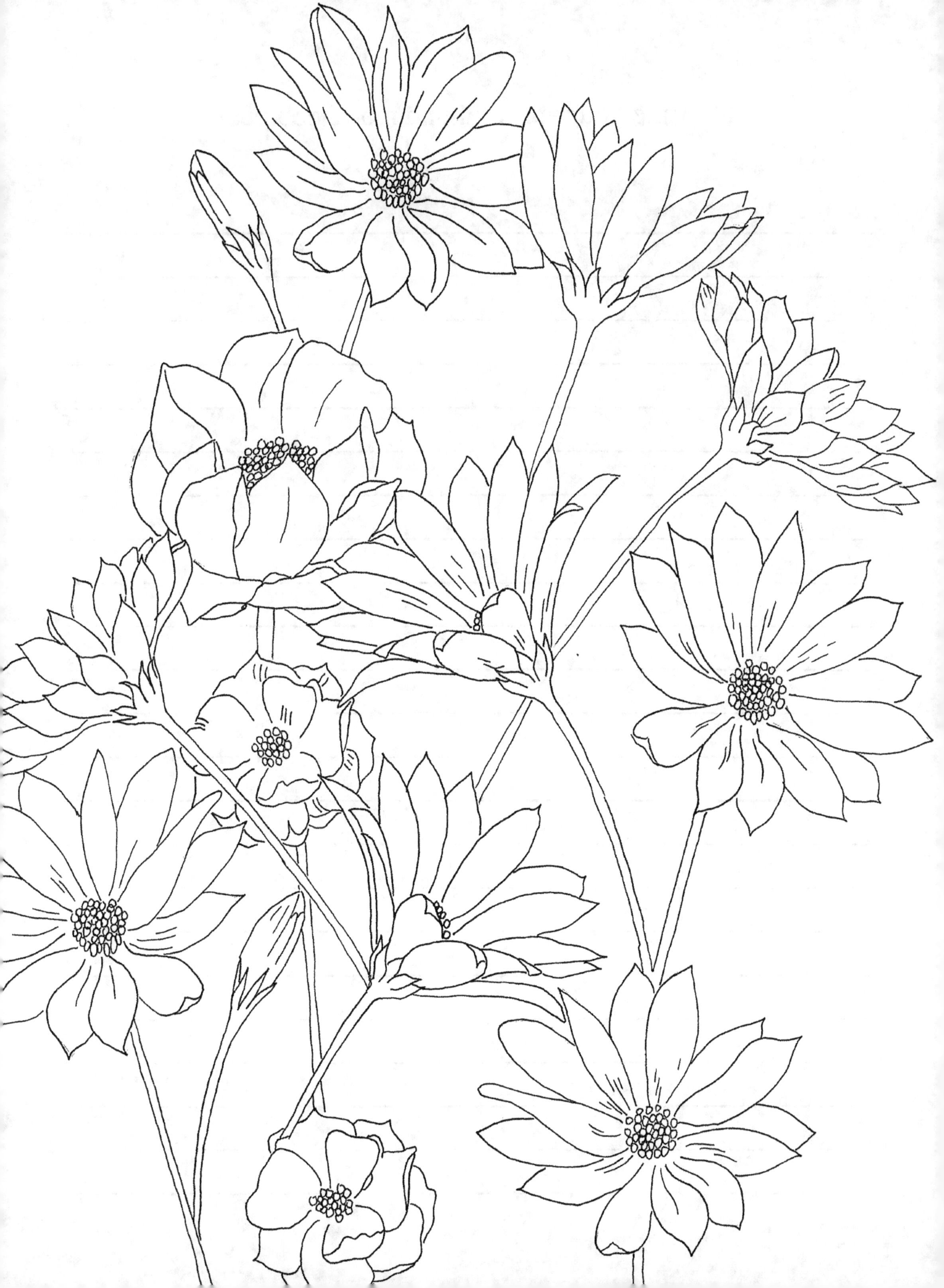

Tune your spiritual and moral compass.

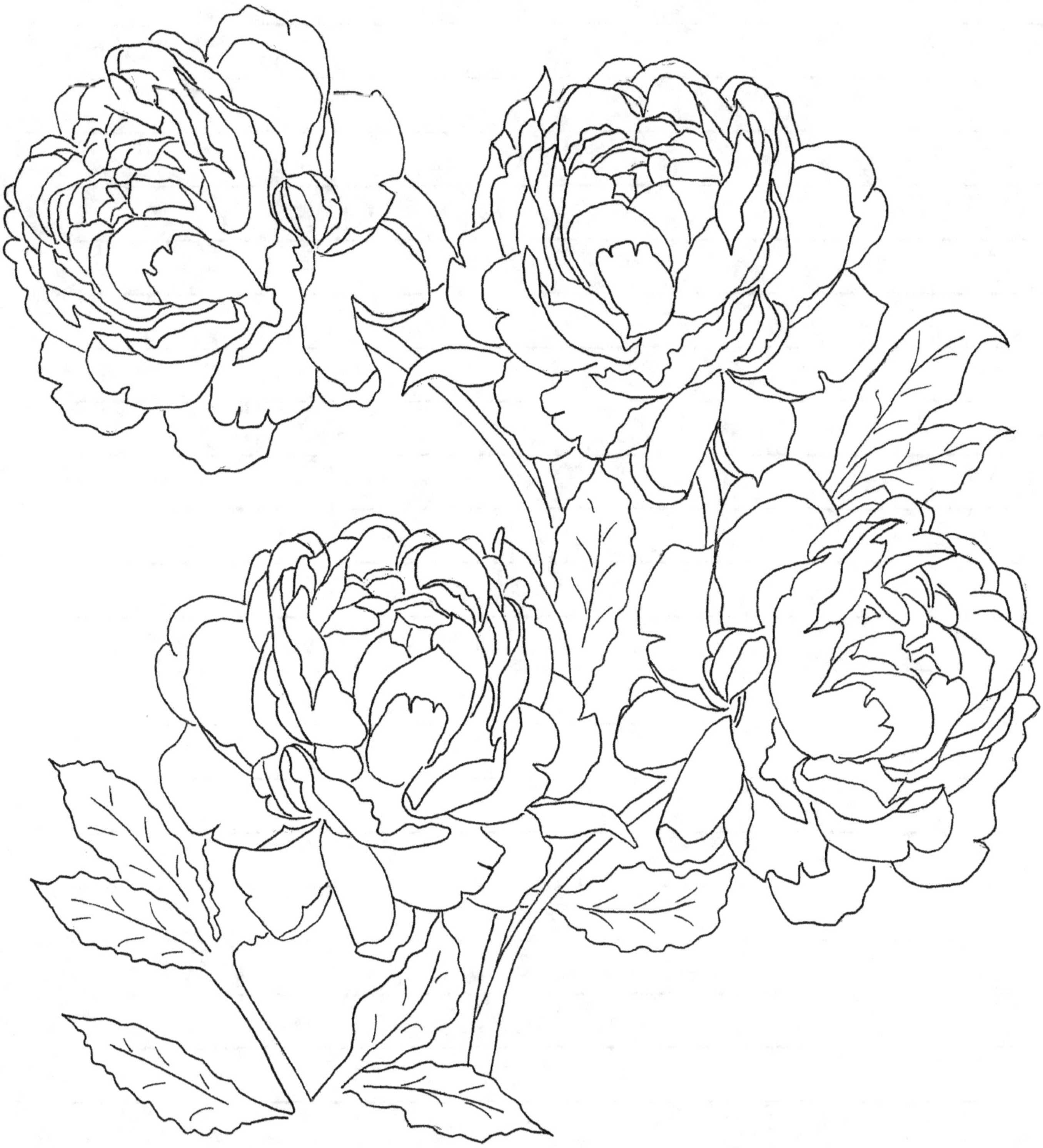

Clear your mind in your journal.

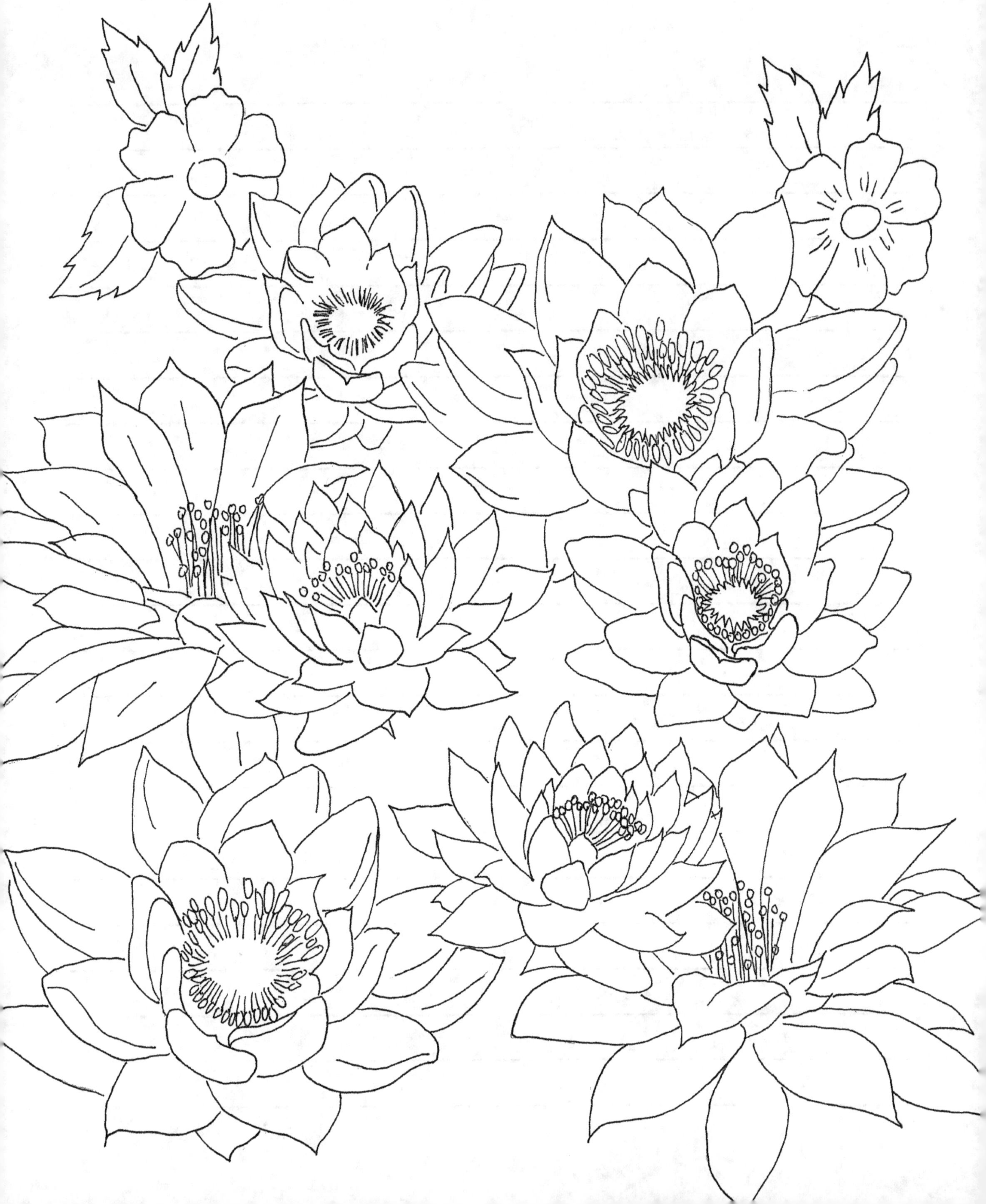

Remember where you have come from in your journal.

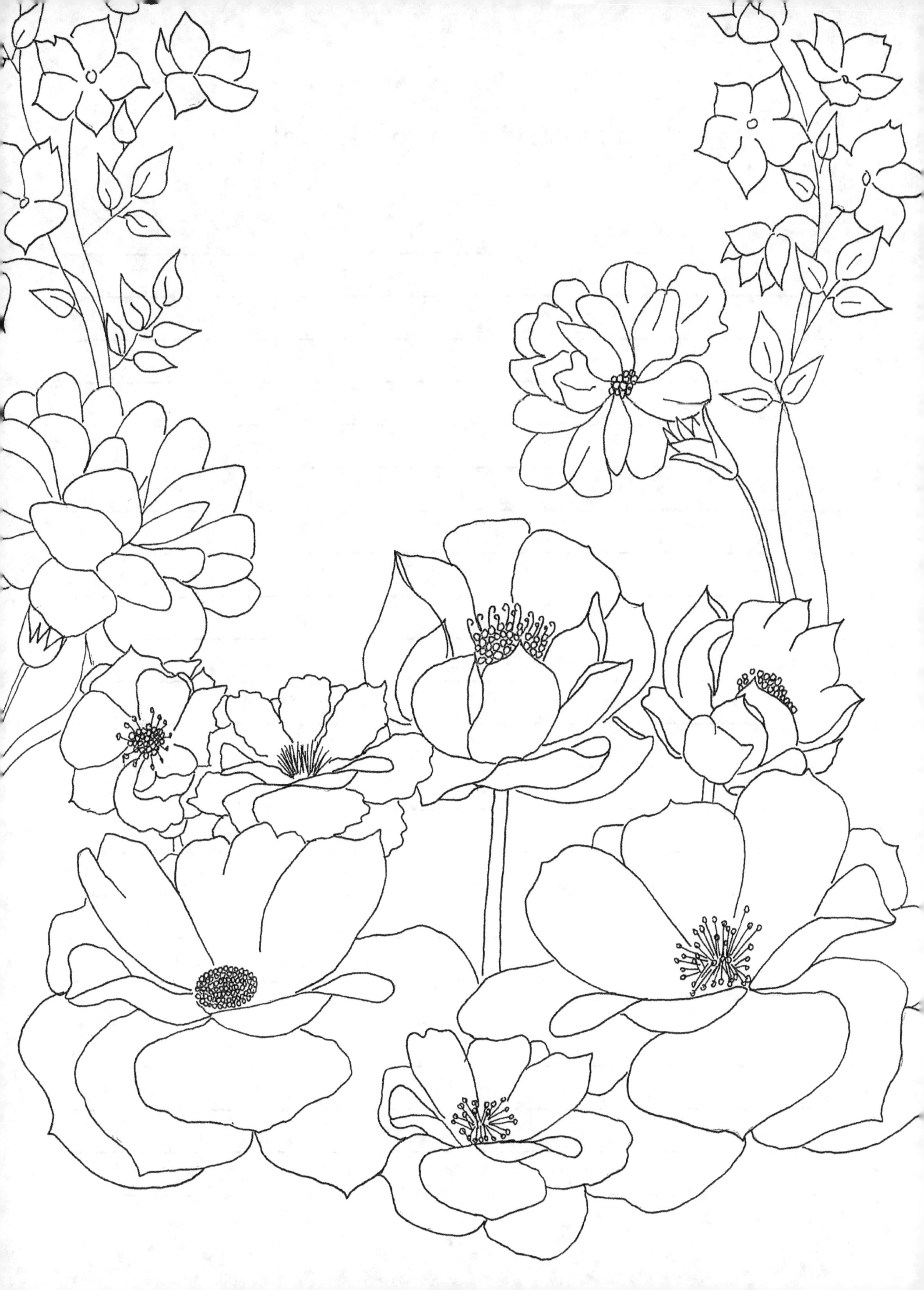

Capture ideas in your journal.

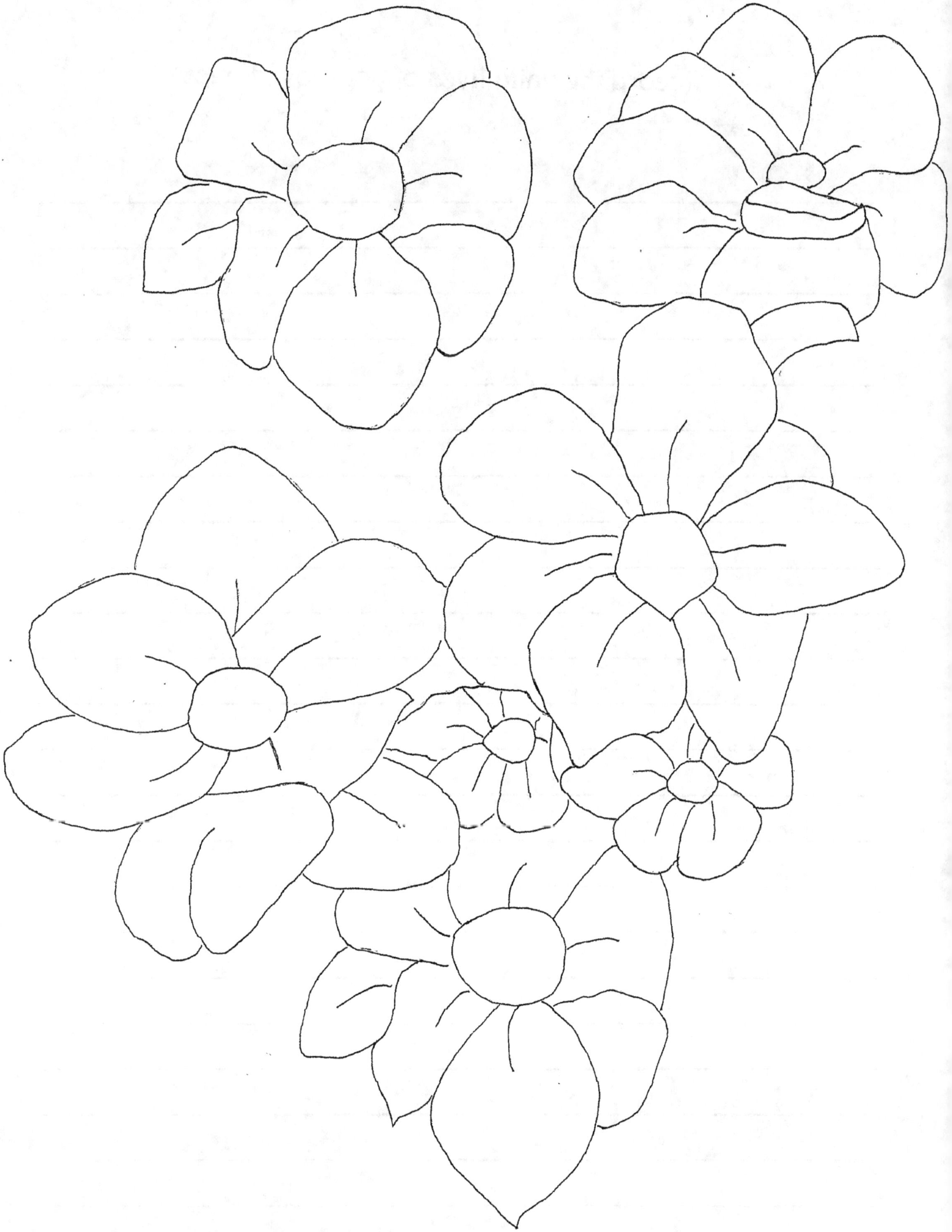

Record the daily lives of your loved ones.

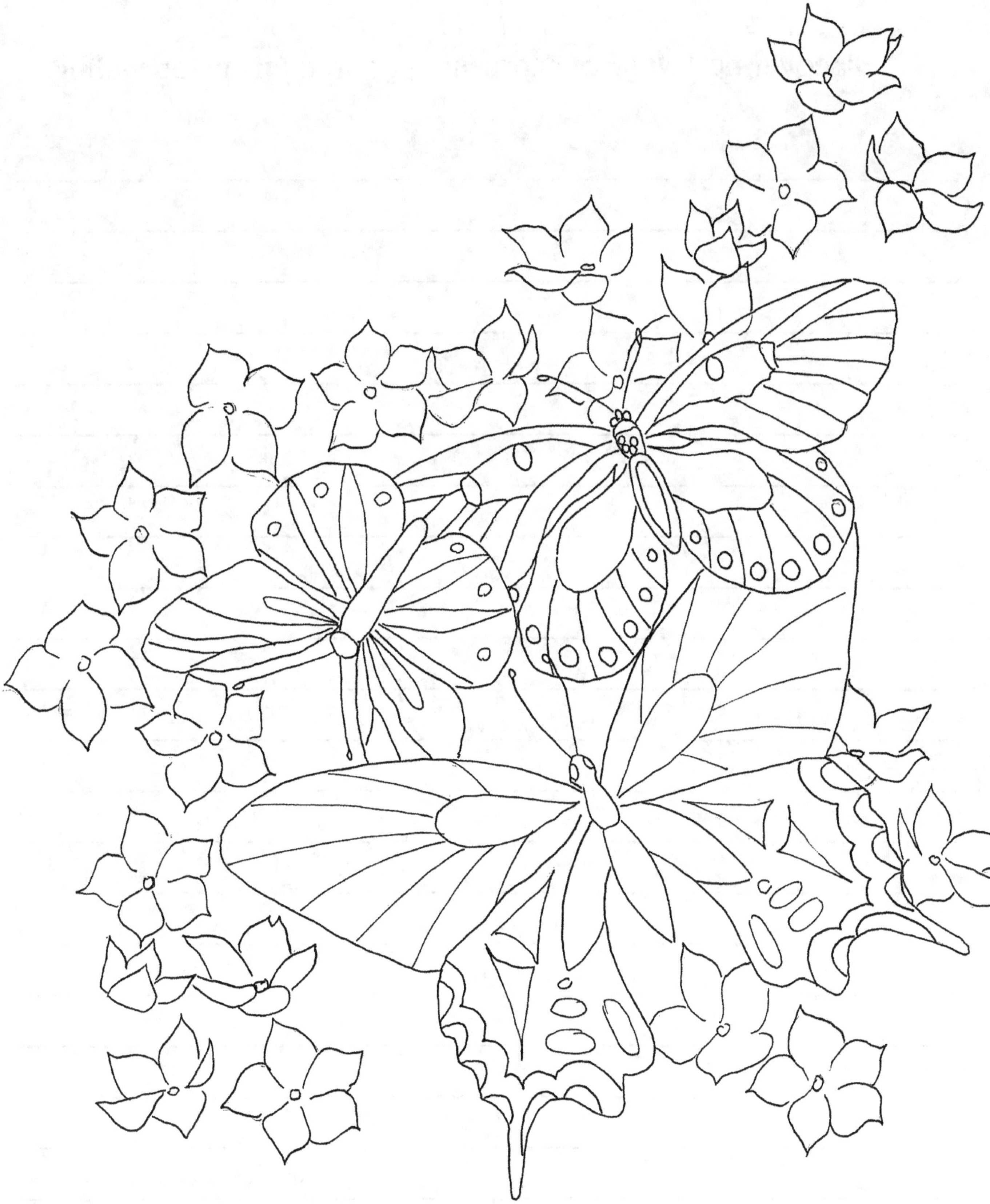

Discover new ways of expressing yourself from journaling.

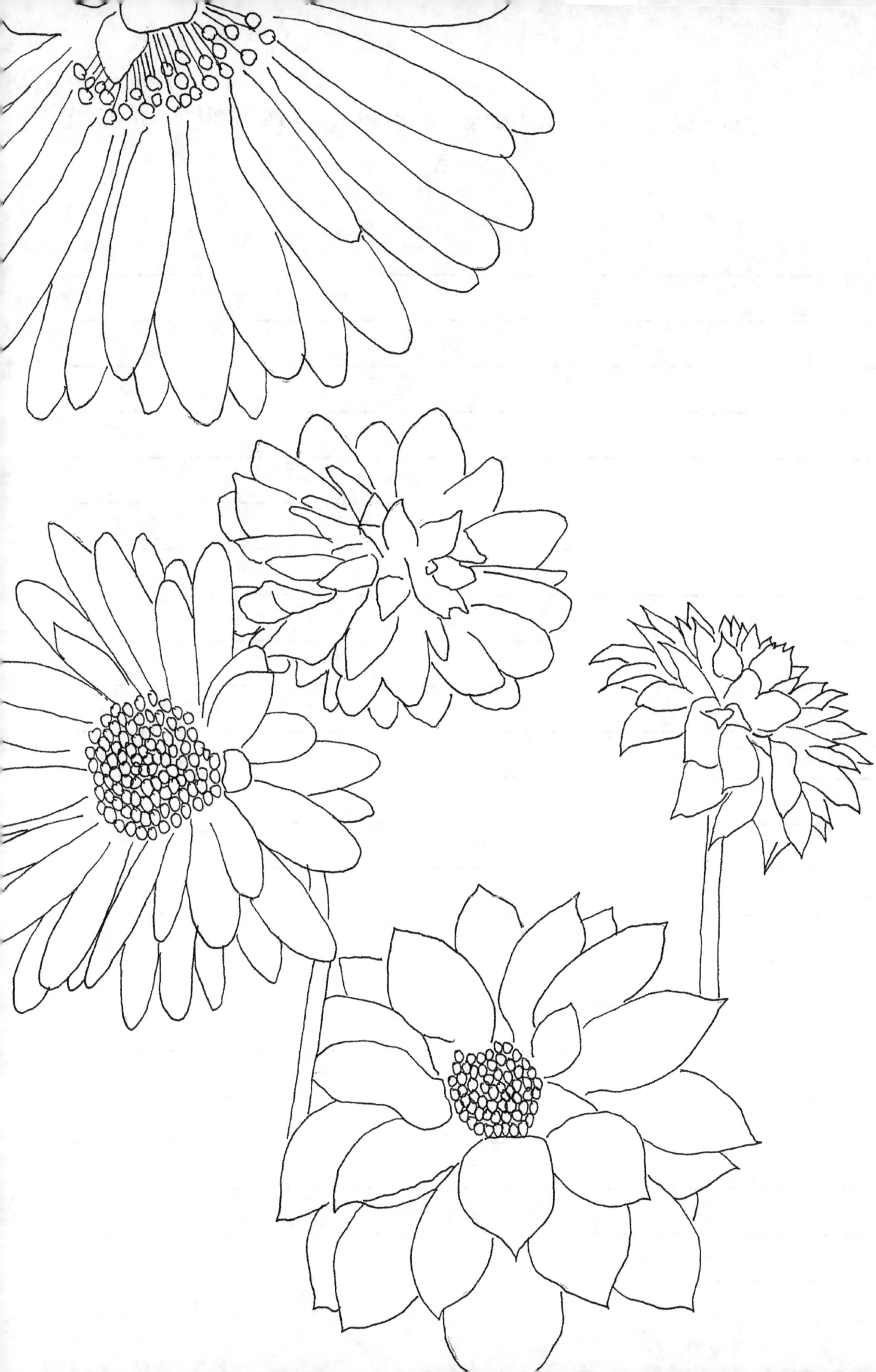

Give yourself some well-deserved moments of reflection in your journal.

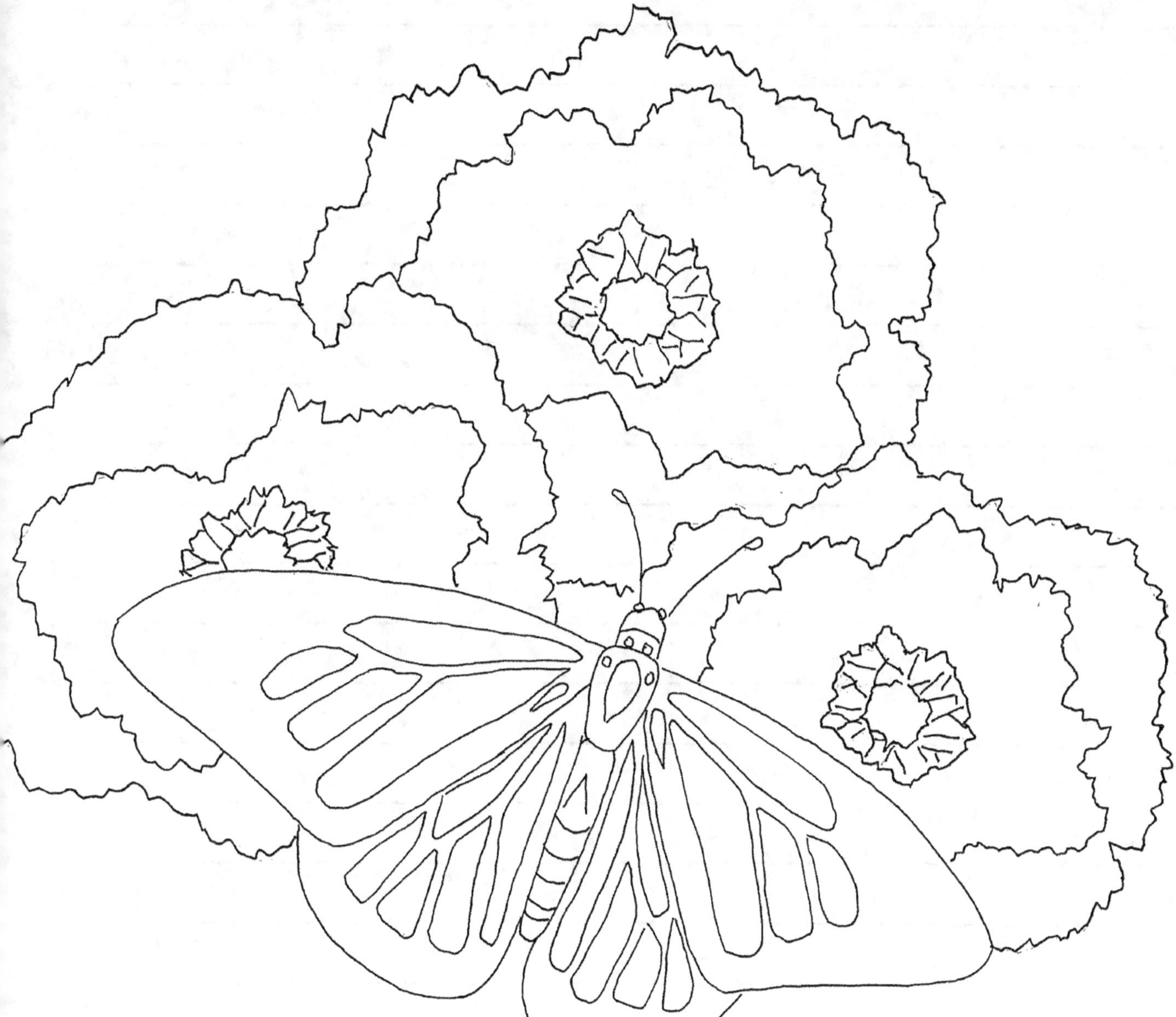

Count your calories in your journal.

www.ingramcontent.com/pod-product-compliance
Lightning Source LLC
Chambersburg PA
CBHW081134180526
45170CB00008B/3100
9781523478255